I, Nadja, and Other Poems

I, Nadja, and Other Poems

Susan Elmslie

Brick Books

Library and Archives Canada Cataloguing in Publication

Elmslie, Susan
        I, Nadja, and other poems / Susan Elmslie.

ISBN-13: 978-1-894078-53-5
ISBN-10: 1-894078-53-5

I. Title.

PS8559.L62I63 2006   C811'.54   C2006-902306-9

We acknowledge the Canada Council for the Arts, the Government of
Canada through the Book Publishing Industry Development Program
(BPIDP), and the Ontario Arts Council for their support of our
publishing program.

   Canada Council   Conseil des Arts   Canadä
for the Arts   du Canada   ONTARIO ARTS COUNCIL
                                                          CONSEIL DES ARTS DE L'ONTARIO

The author photograph is by Danica Meredith, Aperture Solutions.

The book is set in Minion and Tahoma.

Design and layout by Alan Siu.

Printed by Sunville Printco Inc.

Brick Books
431 Boler Road, Box 20081
London, Ontario N6K 4G6
www.brickbooks.ca

For Wes, who went there with me

Contents

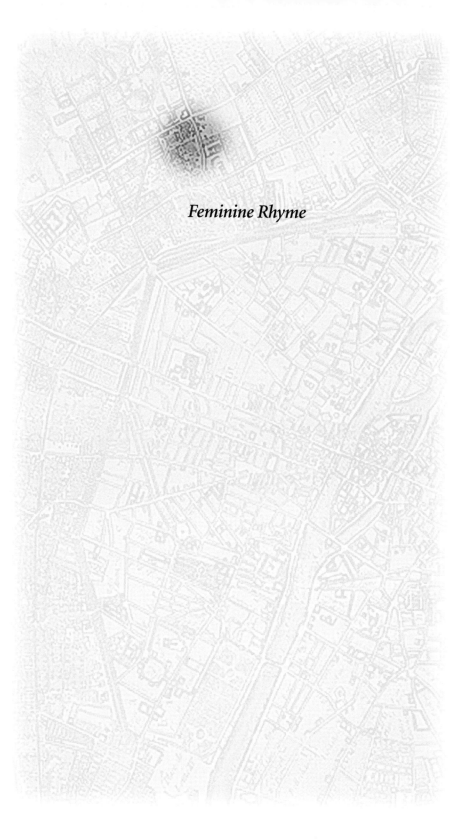

Feminine Rhyme

Pomegranate

My first—
at the Formica dinette set
in your mother's kitchen,
where we'd spent whole days
making cakes in your Easy-Bake oven,
amazed all it took was a light bulb.
One autumn afternoon, sometime between
the Jerry Lewis Telethon
and the Miss Universe Pageant,
you cut the rind in half.
The knife stagy red
like the blade in horror flicks that punishes
the teenagers for making out.
On the cutting board the fruit,
two halves of a brain
that thought only of love.

Inspired by Operation you said, let's try
toothpicks. All the rainy hours we'd passed
extracting tiny bones, wrenches, trying not to
set off the buzzer that lit
the patient's nose
were training for pomegranates.

With practice we discovered
how to tear the rind, carefully
peel away the bitter packaging that makes
your teeth feel like popsicle sticks, and take
whole sections of the seeds at once. The juice barb-
wiring all the creases in our palms, dripping
towards the wrists. Like this,
every time I indulge. I eat your half
and think of you. The patience, the soft burst.

When blood came—you first,
we commandeered the upstairs bathroom.
You with one foot on the toilet seat

and your bum on the edge of the counter,
me sitting on the edge of the tub,
holding the mirror.

Felicity
for Felicity Enayat

Felicity I read a strand of your hair;
A sudden star, it shot through papers, air.
Carefully from your poems I pulled this line,
Peerless alexandrine, sublime feminine rhyme.

Portraits of My Mother

At eighteen my mother sat for a portrait,
and one print turned out so fine,
the photographer displayed it
in the window of his Long Branch shop
(across the street from the hardware store,
where my father later dropped his broom
and dodged a Buick or two to sweep her off her feet).

The best of these prints stood on the top shelf
of the wall unit in our living room.
Each fall I'd place a new glossy of me next to it,
stand back, then demote myself to a lower shelf.
Eyeliner and Polo knockoffs with matching earrings
too garish next to this queen of curds and cream, 1948.

Another print, taken earlier in the sitting, is mine now,
sent to me by my father in a final clean sweep.
You can just see a hint of the white peasant blouse
under a grey wool bolero.
Half a candy apple for a smile.
Eyes ready to deliquesce on cue.

This face is before everything,
before she made a tomb of her sunless bedroom,
grief, a cordate brooch she couldn't unpin.

Seven Letters to My Mother

1. Spendthrift Heart,

When we left off I had a boyfriend
who stole your ATM card, forty dollars, and beat
various happinesses out of me.

I left him on your side of the sea,
flew. I took a leather passport cover, a beaded antique
sweater. I found a younger lover.

His beauty, too, cost me much, Mother: I tried
to forget I was your daughter, inheritor
of the spendthrift heart, consummate gambler.

Those years were bad. I did not write.
It should be known that every night then
was a deep pocket with holes burned through.

I had this dream, I'll tell you,
it changed me. I was back and sleeping
on the couch. A woman climbed down

from the attic. Slight and blonde she resembled me,
and she went to the drawer with the cutlery
in it, and I heard the sound of one knife

distinguishing itself from the rest.
The sound that makes is fear.
She came around the corner, the dagger

before me, and I woke, sat up straight,
calling, "Who are you?"
Fear, the sound that makes, late at night

in an empty room.
What I learned that night will have to wait
for another letter. I'll write soon.

2.   Forgive me, Mom,

I stole your yellow cotton rib-knit vest,

your Bulova 10K gold-filled watch
(& had it fixed, cleaned, and fitted with a custom-made band
to show off *my* wrist).

I took, as well, one filigree earring
that I broke trying on, and meant to have fixed, sneak
it back into your smoke-stained jewellery chest
before it was missed.   I still have it

the black diamond loose in my own chest,
for shame.

A hopeless case

I rummaged in your closet, waist deep.
Sometimes there, I even fell asleep, drunk
on the fumes of things that were not mine.

I emerged once with your wedding portrait, what a find!
Hung it on the wall, pathetic shrine to the doomed couple.
Did you wince when you saw it? you never said a thing.

I found a dildo in your dresser, but did not take it.   Just
finding it burned
my fingers.   I lay off your things

for some time, then.   We kept each other
guessing.   You, you never came into my room
without knocking.   Your searching was implicit.

To come clean at last: I've my eye on the gold-leaf tea set
with the rococo ladies in pink dresses
and the gentlemen in powdered wigs.

I also stole one of your wigs.

3. Other People's Mothers

visit them in jail, give them a pair of Levis
and a carton of smokes for Christmas

have pet names for their children
wink

have the gift of the gab
do small talk like it was coke,

the lines laid out before them
and all afternoon to kill

walk you through things
spill the beans

4. Fortune Cookie

Some mothers' daughters ride the rides.
Some mothers' daughters make beautiful brides.

5. Carry On

We're terrified, both of us: you
of staying put, me
of moving. Or is it the other way
around? Is that what your shuffle is,
part get me out of here, part
where in hell do you think
you're taking me? Just
down the street, Mom. We'll visit.
I'm always in the belly
of the great white shark
of the skies, 747, moving
again, farther away from you.
Change, because it scares me.
What's the alternative? Live
in the bowels of a house you hate,
have hated for forty years.
Stubbing your life on the same
threshold. Shit, I give up
everything, at least twice
a day. I pack it in,
pack it perfectly
in boxes and cases.
I hire other people to help me do it.
Everything gets done, move on.
Or dig your heels in.
We're not the only ones, Mom,
clinging to each other
at the Bon Voyage party.
You give me stationery,
I give you a carry on.

6. Clasp

Watching my baby girl nuzzle,
tugging on my nipple, her tongue
undulating like a sea anemone,
I know I must have felt bliss
at your breast.
No hiding from each other then.
You nursed me between your ripe sheets,
lavishly, grudgingly, the last of your babies.
Later, when you had to change in front of me,
you'd turn your back to slip into your bra,
one arm first and then the other,
straps finding their place in the deep grooves
on your freckled shoulders.
Quick with the clasp
because my eyes gave you no rest.

7. Pisces, you swim in two directions

No letter for some time.
Frustration kept me from sending them
when they go unacknowledged,
when I meanly imagine them piled, gathering dust
in the dead-letter office of your mind.
Each bright stamp glazing over
like the eyes of fish washed up on the beach.
Yes, melodramatic.
I felt it.

Hunger abates when the body's denied
food or contact; we stumble
on for some time, throttling its alarms.
You used to rip the batteries out of the smoke detector
when the broiling cod set the red eye shrieking.

Apparently I am still my own child.

But now bad news comes
almost as a relief, makes it easier
to cast out another line
so to speak. The doctor gave your silence a name:
Alzheimer's—a kind of organized forgetting.

When did it start?
Each of us swimming in two directions
like the symbol for our sign of the zodiac,
and the fish in the song I'd beg you to sing
when I was three: *swim said the mama fish, swim*
if you can—
This moment

I'm rounding up memories
scattered as the beads of a broken choker
and as luminous:
a diver leaping from the lip of a cliff
105 feet high in Acapulco,
where you honeymooned with Dad;

your baby squinting into the sun
for a photograph on the sidewalk
of the new subdivision;
sisters-in-law laughing over an all-night game of cards
at the kitchen table, rum & coke and smoke
hanging in the air with the bawdy talk;
and after Dad left, summers
browning your shoulders on the front porch
with a detective mystery or Linda Goodman's *Sun Signs*.

This moment I swim to you.

Failed Sonnet for My Father

I know you're tired waiting for the first snow.
You talk of going when there are leaves
still on the trees; today a record high
of sixteen. Yesterday a whitewashed sky
told me maybe you were fixing to go.
There will never be a rhyme or season
to make this all right. What am I thinking?
You ache to race beyond this winking light,
and I am only twenty-seven, hold tight
to my hand — with nicotine it's trembling
like yours was that day in the ICU
we pretended I was just cutting school.
I hold onto you like an unopened present.
I don't know where the time went.

Banditos

Her mother dreams the highway past
the border into Mexico, the pregnant
landscape, the bruised sky. The car
windows fitted with screens and
the husband, wire and sweat. Bodies
heavy with fatigue twitching into sleep, very
soupy as dreams are and suddenly.
There are banditos finding the car
and screens easily slit like the sleeping
throats, and the husband's bloated
wallet matters its way out of her mother's dream.

When they come to this stretch of highway,
her mother is adamant. She will not hunker down
to have her throat slit by banditos, she will not
stand for these screens, or for stopping at all,
unless it is in a half-way respectable motel, where,
when she is awakened by bad dreams, there
is only an iguana clinging to the damp drapes, and
the sound of her husband's snores.

She dreams her mother
is awake in this motel, and happy
she stood by her fears, though it is difficult
because the husband matters and the wallet because
this is a second honeymoon, is the wire
holding his retreating body to hers. She sees
this is necessary, the ocean, the smouldering, the banditos.
For her mother standing in the bathtub
with a wire hanger and a will of stainless steel it matters it matters.

Good Fortune Is Coming Your Way

Found it on Pine Avenue not far from the hospital,
this tortoise-shell claw hair clip,
the kind I call the stegosaurus style.
No chipped teeth and made in France,
sturdier than those Dollarama ones
that break apart at the spring
if you haven't got baby fine hair,
if your hair has volume like mine.
I've cracked apart more of those cheapo clips
than fortune cookies and I buy those by the bag.
You would make a good lawyer
was my first fortune the day I found this clip.

I disinfected it. Used bleach
and now it's clean.
Somehow I was more concerned about
the oils on it from somebody's head
than I was about it being sidewalk dirty.
When people are walking around wearing face masks
you can get a little paranoid.
That word extinct keeps coming into my head.

Tearjerker

Our beauty was a sickly child.
We fed her syrup from a measuring spoon,
pills. The pink she liked okay. The yellow and green
karate-chopped her tongue
even when she took them
crushed in jam.
Skinny as a Q-tip
and hated meat.
Hard to get anything past
those lips except maybe
ice cream, ginger ale, potato chips.
Viruses played with her.
When infection set in, to swallow was to swallow
a bowling ball. Said her ears ticked and stuttered
like her tap shoes like the CB
in our custom van—breaker breaker
we got us another tonsil & inner ear fandango.
Fever's 105.
The van skittered and halted like a ladybird
in a jar, stop light stop the night
the doctor smelling of clean laundry
stuck her with a needle and she was quiet for a while.
It's what you don't know
afterwards tears you up inside.
At home, a bathtub full of ice cubes
to get the temperature down.
We held her, rubbing out the cold
and for a while she shook mercy me
like an addict needing a fix, fever-wild.
With her pageant winnings
we had the bathroom tiled.

Dainty

I'm tired of apologies.
If you say anything this time
make it a word you can pick up with a toothpick.
Embroider on the shoulder of a Givenchy gown.
A word like acupuncture for sadness.

Pearls concentrate light.
Small, cultivated. Or a Lalique butterfly,
something with filigree. In a box
no bigger than a lozenge. A fracture
is eased by the balm of dainty, applied
to the wrist like a tennis bracelet.

In the supermarket I can buy Dainty Rice.
(Wearing sunglasses, a peau-de-soie wrap,
elbow-length gloves, my going away outfit.) Kept
very far from the rat poison and lye.

I'm tired of apologies.
Give me the lunula of my finger nails after a manicure.
Something I can slip into painlessly
like vintage silk.
And dainty, dainty.
Even the dungeon walls will perspire.

Smile me up, Jackie

like the time we scrambled
across marbled ice to Crescent Street
two Keystone Cops, falling
on our Bundt cakes.
Then, on the way home,
rapping out blurbs à la Don Pardo
for unlikely TV pilots:
"She's a hard-nosed Wall Street lawyer;
He's a displaced Eskimo woman. Together,
they're *Fishing for Clues.*"

Smile me up,
like the time we did the Safety Dance,
celebrating sheer goofiness—the reckless
pole vault over a rough patch of irony.

Sometimes, clarity.
Like the time angels escaped
our mouths, hovered in the corners
of your small room, beating the last light
out of a late winter afternoon.

You witnessed me
cast my love out to the wrong men,
lick my wounds, start again.

    Smile.
I have learned some die-hard love
from you.
Like the time it was clear I was history;
your eyes made blue rain
so mine didn't have to.

Meanwhile

Now it is my turn: blue rain for you,
though I know you have had your own
record floods all
over the map this year.

Not to make light.

The snows of March
are pathetic; winter's last-
ditch effort to hold us under.
Our superheroes live in far off cities,
making necessary such things
as correct postage, standby.
Now your love has gone
and emptied his pockets,
exchanged the Teflon suit
for human skin, disappointed you.
You're shoving passport underwear birth control pills
into a hockey bag. Sitting by the door
like a Lhasa Apso.

As for useful advice, I've got less
than Polonius gathering dust behind the arras.

But to make light.
To be grateful
for the comic relief, the sure gag: banana
peel, hall of identical doors, marbles
landing the sourpuss teacher on his arse. To laugh

friend we need to laugh
when April throws things out every window, applaud
when she shakes winter like an old rug, washes
her hands, and brings out the jewellery.

Meanwhile, can I do this
for you, can I
come over with my two hands help you

✓ pick up
your laundry, ✓ change
the sheets, ✓ scrub the tub, ✓ turn
off the taps.

Shave
for Jennifer Williams

A snapshot of four girls at the mall food court:
Michelle wearing perfect hair and Esprit Sport,
Karen trying to eat a burger through new braces.
Serene Mercan, leaning in to the group.
    And Jennifer, giddy
    off to one side. Eyes wide,
    laughing so big you can see
    the silver in her molars.

I took the picture.
And before this another, and
another: We're in gym class, grade eight,
skinny teens in school tees, hugging our chests,
stretching our hamstrings out
in the field, waiting
for our turn at the long jump.
Late autumn brisk and the gym
teacher's whistle barely within earshot.
Suddenly Michelle points, aghast,
at Jennifer's ankle, sliced
and newly scabbed over,
dark red. Jennifer laughs, and says
Cut it shaving. A scratch.
We hug ourselves tighter,
gooseflesh shudder, and
our shrill gag-me squeals
draw the gym teacher near.

After hearing about the car accident
I couldn't shave without thinking of her
in random seasons of decay.
Now I'd see her flesh loosening around her bones.
Now a skull, theatrical,
white under a cap of brittle autumn leaves.
Laughing molars.

When, a few years later, I sliced
a nickel-sized patch from my knee-cap,
my hand slapped over the white sting.
The release of tears because Jennifer would never
carelessly cut herself shaving again.
And for the luxury of such mundane accidents—
hot water suddenly steaming on my back,
nicks and near misses, my own
good luck.
For what takes us
within a hair's breadth of irrecoverable
and leaves us in one piece. Escape
by the skin of our teeth and other fragile boasts.
And then, too, for what is *enough*.
A razor's lip, radial strip, arithmetic
divides the living from the ghosts.

Every time I shave
we're stretching our legs on that splash of grass
cold as a grave.
When the gym teacher hushed our squeals,
Jennifer plunked down on the grass and casually
stretched her long body into the hurdler's stretch,
that red *whatever* gash
grinning above the white ankle sock
her mother last weekend had washed and bleached.

Free Climbing Rhyme for Lori

I remember your shoulders
muscled and golden, smooth
hinges bolted to your
sinewy frame, core-strong

you were training to
climb mountains, to endure
high altitudes, to carry
all the necessary gear

for solitary treks. Before
leaving you'd scatter your
mom's ashes, her last
wish, your past tumbling

like scree into the
vast forgiving sea.
Did I see your hands
pull in parts of yourself—

shoulder blade, clip, agate?
Your eyes knew wind,
the need for self-
rescue equipment.

I came away thinking
about compassion, about oxygen
emergency masks, what we
must give to ourselves

before we can give
it to another. How
ironically we sometimes need
to go where air

is rarefied to learn
to breathe, to forget
what we've learned. I
wonder how you'll return

shaved, thin, all pelvis
and shin, burnished tin plate
what you've shouldered left at the gate
if the gate will be open

Convalescent

I think: if I am dying then I will want to go to the beach.
Someone will prop me up on a *chaise longue*
(I even like hearing the words *chaise longue*)
under a canvas umbrella snapping like rigging in the wind,
facing the ocean, of course. I'll drink Evian
(liquid yoga, my friend calls it) from a glass
with a bendy straw. I see a hand,
not my own, supporting that glass
and another adjusting the pillow behind my head.
Then my friend begins to slice me an Alabama peach.

What does this mean? I worry. I'm sure it's neurotic
to devour convalescence as a genre.
It's not so bad, my friend says to me:
It means you are always getting better.
It means you are already past the worst.

Lump

The gowns have got better over the years.
They used to be papery. Putting them on
made you feel a little like fast food.
Now at least they're soft washed cotton, though
this one smells exactly like a taco shell.
I've pulled my arms out of it, and am lying on my back,
staring at the underbellies of wooden tropical fish
on a mobile over my head. Two of each kind, I see:
a pair of blue and white ones with purple flashes,
two seaweed and amber ones, a fiery orange and red pair. Only
one pink one, though. Rare fish low in the murky water.
It's pea-sized, the doctor is saying, picking up my hand
and pressing my fingers to it, deep
in my left breast beside the nipple, *at 8:00.* She lands my hand there
with such force I feel like I am pressing the elevator button
for the second time. I'm reminded
also, more vaguely still, of someone I saw smooshing a dog's nose
in poop on the living room carpet, the words *bad dog.*
I never would have found that, I say, partly in defence, partly
in awe. My fingers rest dutifully there a moment,
as if I were making a pledge.
Then I scuttle upright on the table, wrap the robe around me.
Any history in your family? the doctor wants to know.
My granny's sister lost a breast to cancer.
Then there are quick calculations related to my cycle,
caffeine consumption, age. My mind
starts to shut down with the introduction of the words,
ultrasound, biopsy, Urgent Breast Clinic.
I've gone under, swimming in my deep blue robe,
my head sounds like a seashell, a churning undertow.
The walk to the bus stop I catch myself involuntarily
saying words out loud: *never; tired; clay,* now and then
punctuating my disbelief with hand gestures
straight out of silent film. So the crazy ladies
are just worried, I intuit, jabbing
the air with its unseen buttons.
Later, on the phone long distance, my mother

tells me that she wonders whether Auntie's lump
didn't come about because, years earlier, she caught
her breast in the wringer washer real bad.
How such things may be related who can predict?
Earlier this summer my neighbour chased off an addict
who was at the recycling bins on his back deck,
fishing for returnable empties in the murky 4 a.m. light. I woke up
to hear the young securities dealer warning the interloper:
I'll give you a lump—I'll lump ya if you come back here.
Months ago, waking up in the dark to this hard-boiled threat, I laughed
out loud, easily, safe under layers: night-gown, down comforter.

Cyst

This time I get two gowns.
One you're supposed to put on as if you walked into it
like a doctor scrubbed for the OR,
or (as in my case) a sleepwalker. In slow-mo,
automatic pilot, the schlimazel's alternative to fight or flight.
The other gown you wear like a robe, I suppose
to make you feel less vulnerable. One more layer
between your tender self and the world
of latex gloves and machinery.
I'm also given a big plastic bag
to put the clothes for the top half of my body in,
and my purse. To keep everything together.

In the waiting room Rachel's doing her best
to make conversation to distract me, capably performing
one of the two great roles for friends. (The other
is to focus us on what we'd rather not face,
when, heaven forbid, the time is right.) Time

telescopes and we're soon peering with the doctor
at the ultrasound image of a black pearl,
not ragged, *thank you*, not casting an ominous black shadow,
thank God, not solid. 98% certain, the doctor is, that it's just
a cyst.

So where do I go from here? Unclench my fists;
subtly extol the benefits of regular breast examinations
and then (in the privacy of my room)
get to know all my lumps and broken spokes;
breathe a prosaic sigh of relief; suddenly buoyant, tell jokes;
cast my own dark shadow of doubt (*2% uncertain?*); reflect
on the fate of those not so lucky: cousins, sisters, aunts (make a donation?),
weep; slip out of these robes, tuck my shirt into my pants,
go home, sleep.

First Apology to My Daughter

I birthed you like an animal,
soft flanks rising with calm
deepening breaths, brown eyes indifferent
to the hands of well-meaning helpers.
After hours of baffled pushing
and an enfilade of sutures, I surrendered
you to the nursery, just
a couple of hours,
while my body sunk into the mattress
like a slug sinks back into the earth
after its encounter with a shovel.
I didn't know the harried nurse
would think it best not to wake me
to feed you. You yearning
for your first milk
while I dozed
on some far off platform.
That you would tighten
the coil of your body trying to burst
the seam of your swaddling blanket, and cry
that tremulous muscular cry
and me out of earshot. Cry
long enough to give up on crying.
What darkness then, in the fluorescent hours
of the maternity ward while
I taught you the ferocity of hunger.

Marie Curie's Cookbooks

Every day for three years you cooked up
a twenty-kilo cauldron of pitchblende
stirring with an iron pole
in the shed that doubled as a lab
behind the School of Industrial Physics and Chemistry.
With Pierre you shouldered
one day into the next; hope's salve
eased the pains of separating, analyzing
the better part of a mine slag-heap
under a cracked, leaking glass roof. Aching
feet rooted to a dirt floor. *A cross between a stable
and a potato shed*, chemist Wilhelm Ostwald said,
having travelled from Germany to meet you and Pierre
and see where you worked.

You boiled down tonnes of pitchblende,
effectuated thousands of crystallizations
to extract a mere decigram of almost pure radium chloride
so as to calculate radium's atomic weight,
proving the existence of something theretofore unseen. New
elements, decay and transformation more fantastic
than the gold dreams of alchemy.

ह৺

Did you make Ève and Irène take stir-shifts
at the pot of salt-water taffy, on a Sunday,
when you weren't at the cauldron in the shed
but in your own kitchen, *Maman*
in the *foyer*, smelling of cassonade and butter,
embracing your girls
with radioactive arms?
Tucking them in to bed, did you
review the Periodic Table, tell them
Aesop's fables by the light emanating from a radium salt,
the "night-light" you kept at your own bed-side?

When the girls were nearly grown and Albert Einstein
rang the bell to visit, was one of your cracked thumbs
holding the book open to *Kaffekuchen*,
finding the recipe through your slag-heap fatigue
accomplishment enough?

&

More than a hundred years later
at the *Bibliothèque Nationale*
hungry researchers sign a certificate
stating their willingness
to die a little for you, risk
exposure to the radium dusting your skin
like *poudre LeClerc*, fine luminous
particles lodged deep in the binding, spine
of your notebooks, the grain
of your vellum papers, a spilled ink stain.
Your own white bones and blood.

Because we're hungry
for generous portions of joy and grief, to feast
and afterwards break the plates, for
Marie Curie's cookbooks,
to taste flour, confectioner's sugar
with a half-life of 1620 years
on the dog-eared pages
of your *Livre de cuisine*, which,
around dinner time,
we would pause over, try to guess
what dish you might have cooked for Pierre, left
to scorch in the oven, pots pitch-
black, the night he was *adieu*ed
by horse and buggy not far from the Pont Neuf.

George Sand's Wardrobe

A cupboard in the wall of my boudoir
begins a new life
when fitted with shelves;
                    one of them deeper, hinged:
Voilà the secretary where George Sand will write
her first books.
Inclining forward, sitting on my left foot
on one of the Louis XVI chairs
that naughty Aurore dragged
across the herringboned floor,
leaving my first literary scratches,
I like to think.

Grandmother Dupin wouldn't be pleased.
Aurore, to console me you must be properly brought up,
her first words to me (barely four, and puny).
She lifted me out of the carriage
and I was brought in to the manor at Nohant, protected,
removed from the pleuritic rooms and the shadow of improbity
after my father died and my mother, well, continued.
This was Grandmother's boudoir before it was mine.
Her adjoining bedroom, with its *lit à la Polonaise* is
too cold, correct; I'll spend my nights here,
bent over the shelf of my hide-away secretary.
With tobacco and without the Baron
I will sit, dipping my pen, learning
how to begin from these hands, this skin.
These forward shoulders, this storming head of uncoiled hair,
my body at work: happy
travesty of Grandmother's harp,
still in the corner behind me, a proper lady.

It pleases me to sleep in the hammock I've hung
where the velvet divan used to be.

When I die I do not think they will say
George Sand was a great man,

follow my coffin solemnly
in the mist of dear Frédéric's *Marche Funèbre*.
Nor will they bury me in the Panthéon,
that edifice consecrated by Napoléon
to great men from a grateful fatherland.

Make no mistake, she loved
and was loved, left greenness:
walnuts blooming in the *boiserie*, and roses
below the windows. You see—

I made this
wardrobe-secretary, and from this spring
one hundred books, forty thousand letters.
The embraces of lovers.
My profession, to be free.

So I made as well the trousers and waistcoat, fine
all wool worsted, fully-lined—
work which Tailleurs Riche & Fils
respectfully declined.

Feminine epic

Call me the vibrating girl.
My legs shake in my loose jeans
like my dreams of machinery
gone awry: the washer convulsing
out of the closet,
a big stone belly about to split.
Used to be I had the love of Jesus
staccato on my ribs thrummed by an invisible bow.
And moods like accelerated photography:
the seed that breaks through dirt
flower
dying for the freeze frame.
Oh, God, there is some small sorrow in me
quavers at the sight of a perfect lime,
or the straight spine of a sapling girl —
what throat to have a shaking fist in it,
what lungs a-knocking.
Now, before the smallest men, even
my voice forgets I have
pockets with things in them,
a home and no visible scars.
I scope the street for doors to duck into, dark places
to hide where I might see other small eyes
and blink and stretch.

If there's a woman on the street

"I told Blanchette, 'If there's a woman on the street, I'll grab her.'"
—Jean-Paul Bainbridge, convicted for his role in the rape and murder of 22-year-old music student Isabelle Bolduc, perpetrated June 30, 1996, in Sherbrooke

Let her have her hands
on useful instruments: stitch-
ripper, nail file, stiletto. Her voice
a needle to puncture ears.
Let her know how to snap
a knee-cap like a lobster.
Let her know how to kill.

If there's a woman
she has rehearsed her fear, she has
feared the hearse inching up behind her
between the bus stop and home.
She has filled her lungs with fire
to shout Fire! like she's been told.

In her nightmares she has split
a head like a *head*
with an axe like her hand.
She has suspended herself in high places,
spewed lava. *There is no such thing—*

Sputtering. We don't help
her. Give life-25
to the hands that drag her by the hair
smash her head with a pipe
drop her in a ditch at our feet there
was a woman on the street.

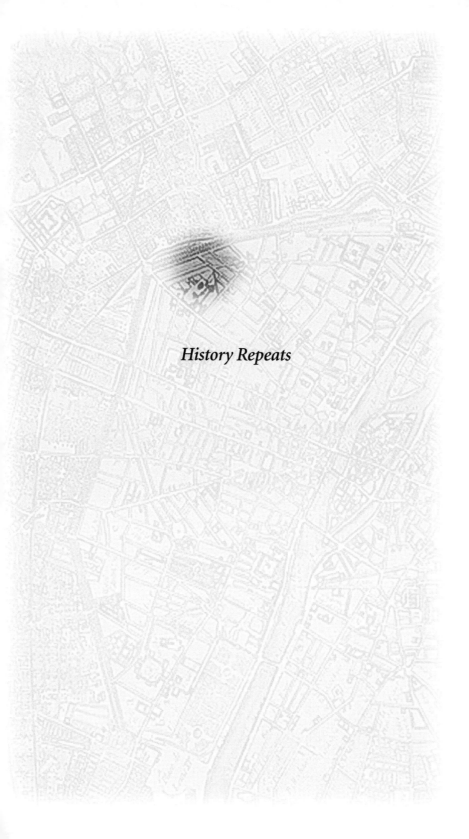

History Repeats

I write

because poetry is to the body as energy is to mass; it lives
in me as in you, and perhaps
because we have little else to give one another, you and I
because history repeats with the cocooning of secrets

because I have loved and hidden it
in cycles sure as Mississippi floods:
stupendous litany of ampersands
it swells and washes and carries the house
away

and to find it again I must describe it
to you

Have you seen the shark's eye glint on my bone-handled knife,
the lime that bleeds May?

The gentle cadence of escape

Snow falling as Chopin's pale fingers
over the notes of a Nocturne, andante,
suspended in listening air. Like you, still
ten paces back, arms outstretched
to arras glistening. "This is so *beautiful*," you say
in the gentle cadence of escape, and windows wink at us
like we're pulling a heist.
  (Before we stumble together
  over snow out cold in the field
    there is a moment
  your mouth tastes sweet, yes
  your mouth tastes sweet

How the litchi came to be

A god found his wife alone with his best archer. Enraged, overtaken with jealousy, he turned the archer into a stone, smooth as the archer's draw, dark as the eye of the hart, small as spite. The wife, crushed by remorse and grief, threw herself down and grasped this small stone, curling up around it in her white nightdress drenched with tears. Her lingering desire transformed her: pale flesh wrapped tightly round a dense dark heart, sweetness of tears. Moved by the intensity of emotion, the god took pity on the lovers, and tucked them into a shell-like cocoon where they could embrace for eternity. The shell warmed and glowed; the lovers' flushed cheeks. This is how the litchi came to be.

Déjà vu

slides into home plate
like a clumsy fat kid,   long after
the field has cleared.
A twinge
and the sun creeps out from behind a cloud
a doorway flasher, the half smile
smoother than Man Ray photographs, the mouth
full of don't know. Just enough
for the hungry snake of a heart
that gulps moments whole.

Four Postcards

A last attempt: the language is a dialect called metaphor.
These images go unglossed: hair, glacier, flashlight.
When I think of a landscape I am thinking of a time.
When I talk of taking a trip I mean forever.

A Valediction Forbidding Mourning Adrienne Rich

With the tongue spell words of love on the body,
your life's story, now, while there's time — there must be
one version where we say what we need to —
and don't ask where we're going. Just the tongue
fleshing out response: inflections of the open heart.
Or will I always be waiting outside your closed door,
sounds from the promenade below an open window
whispering, my own skin glowing phosphorous, breaking wave,
disbelieving *love can't cherish what it can't relax for.*
A last attempt: the language is a dialect called metaphor.

Leon told me I write a good close, and that the poem should begin
where it ends. Like us I suppose. Me living in that space at the end
that says *there's more there's more.* And you, no more
than the colour of air round the mountain at dusk, albescent
trees stretching into sky, birds, chimney smoke slipping
everything slipping now into the dry mouth of night.
Stilling. Goodbye's a coda of clogged pipes that begins even
before the leaf extends palm, before the hand shakes, before
the veins constrict and the heart, the heart burns its name into white.
These images I gloss, here, on my face, in the half-light.

Other revelations wait under my tongue like arsenic.
In London you surprised me, and in Paris and Ottawa
we moved nearer like glasses on a wet counter, dangerous. The need
to steal something from you, a promise, your lying skin.
A long time without you and still I cannot name
all the ways your body haunts mine. Every few nights

white-knuckled November snaps branches like pencils,
the leafless trees within me.
Because, my love, we did sleep spine to spine,
when I think of a landscape I am thinking of a time.

I can get perfect distance between us — maybe
language is what washes the sheets eventually,
snapping on the line, telling us how neat things must be.
Like irony: a man spent eighteen years building a plane, only
to have it crash on its maiden flight, killing him completely.
Some throw themselves into the role of the timeless lover,
believing only in their own ability to endure, endure
and prepare for that chance meeting at an airport bar.
You look at me and I know I have blown my cover.
When I talk of taking a trip I mean forever.

Dark Days

You are more memory than flesh,
like the slip of a thing I was before sex
swelled yearning into hips and breasts. So
I write you a love letter,
which just about leaves me speechless,
the colour of your eyes:
a lump in my throat.
                          It is so many days since
I've lost count.
Now your voice is only snow
falling from the roof.
I have lost your body, my love, lost
much more. Everything
I buy comes with a piece missing,
waitresses conspire to deprive me
of coleslaw or cutlery.

But there you must be
in your part of the world, opening
doors and drawers and taking things on or
off, as you please,
uncorking Chablis. Am I right?

How should I know my morning
if not as your night — my sun
paler than the harvest moon
bursting in the slender window
of a rented room the eve
of your national holiday?

Grand Café de la Paix
for J.E.L.

I was fading away too, part of me
overexposed postcard.
The thought that choked me: it might be years
before your blue eyes.

Away, away.

An accordion player moves in on your absence
too soon.
My sister leaning into me croons
You got it real bad, girl. Then
the tips of her fingers
on my hand.
        Oh
        the light of you:
        awning/ windscreen/ sun/ clean
gone.

Somehow over time Severn Bridge

Severn Bridge. A place I go back to
with a prickling in my bones, sliding
into serous dreams of the August river
lapping at my feet, senses
a-twitch like the snoozing dog's paws,
squeals of children from the lodge
down a ways, crickets
through the open car window
when we slow at the bend. Dusk
that never ends, just slips
on a cooler dress and saunters
into the trees.

        A book slips off my knees: six hours in a Greyhound.
        In my bag two swimsuits and enough
        paperbacks to pass ten days on the dock
        where Jojo lost her first gold ring
        and we had to sing like Morrissey
        to get a smile, ah *there.*

Seems the seriousness of my relationships was determined
by which boys I'd bring up there,
and whether we'd sneak out
through the moth-jewelled sliding screen door at night
to make love on the weather-beaten back porch
or break up in the stalled motorboat,
sunburned, thirsty, ears ringing from speeding
to the centre of the lake.

        CFNY breaking into static, we take our exit
        off the highway, my sister and I.
        The trees come closer.
        My cupped hand out the window, head back,
        eyes closed, I am thinking of Chas,
        his whole body poised
        for *sniff* the first *sniff* of

gulp lake air.
From the bend, where he'd jump
out of the pickup, he'd race us
and win.

Swing bridge arabesques over the Severn,
locks in place over the river's glissade.
Somehow over time this delicate *pas de deux*.

Docents

The dead are docents
hovering at the thresholds
of our lives,
one hand cradling their telephone to God
the other beaming light on our beautiful mistakes.

Call it love. They'd keep us
from making a mess of things
if that, too, wasn't part of it:
not the light or master stroke only,
but the chiaroscuro, the idiosyncratic
composition, sublime accident,
the equivalent of Jackson Pollack's
splatters and drips on our best self-portrait.

And the way we take in beauty,
sometimes like a veil lifted
sometimes like a hammer dropped on the foot.
Our bravado, too, is endearing.
What they missed while they were here
they now study, their mind's eye
a slide show of the highlights.

It's a long shift. But they don't rest
on the bench at the centre of the gallery.
They recall what it's like
to stand behind the ropes,
to have one's view blocked
by folks who've pushed their way to the front.
They've wandered the entire exhibit, they know
the arrangement inside out. But nothing fades
into the background for them. Each detail
of face and figure, of colour and line is
resplendent. *This room is closing,*
they'll one day tell us. *Proceed to the exit.*

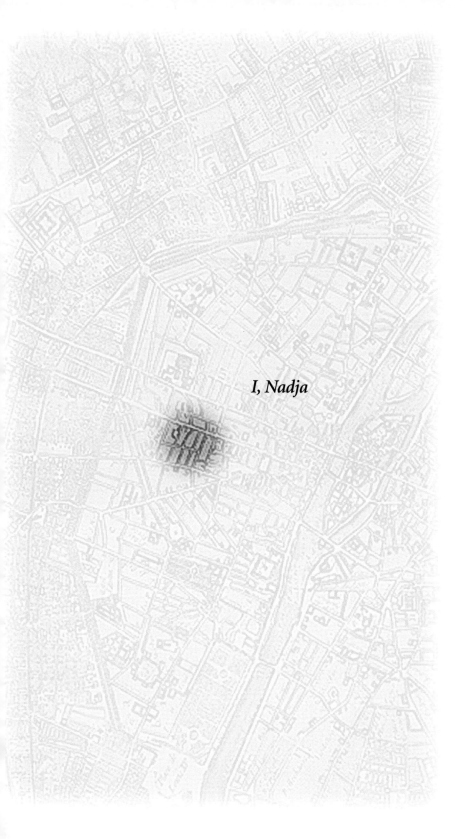

I, Nadja

All I know is that this substitution of persons stops with you, because nothing can be substituted for you, and because for me it was for all eternity that this succession of terrible and charming enigmas was to come to an end at your feet.
You are not an enigma for me.
I say that you have turned me from enigmas forever.

— André Breton, *Nadja*

To please them must we follow the unknown woman step by step, to illuminate her up to the ankle? The worn-down heels, the mud, the bleeding foot—humble and precise evidence—would touch someone.
No. I shall follow the wake in the air, the trail in the water, the mirage in the pupils."

— Claude Cahun, "The Invisible Adventure"

I cannot be reached.
— Nadja
(*Nadja*; also quoted in Pierre Naville's memoir, *Le Temps du suréel*)

Dedication

On the grounds of the Sainte Anne hospital in Paris's fourteenth
district trim streets and gardens are named after artists and writers
who've dealt with mental illness, either first hand, as with Van Gogh,
Camille Claudel and Antonin Artaud, or second-hand, as in one
notable case: witness *Allée André Breton*—an alley, complete with
industrial-size garbage bin overflowing with black trash bags.

I have to wonder at the irony that Breton ended up with an alley
named after him here. The general public might not know that his
surrealist muse Nadja was actually confined behind these walls in
March 1927 (when the buds on the magnolia trees, on the green
outside the frame, were just splitting their seams) before being
moved to another hospital and, sometime later, to yet another
nearer her family in Lille, where she died.

No street bears her real or adopted name. Until now, just a book,
his. Which she likely never read.

Other traces of her are elusive and fragmentary: kept under wraps
by her family to protect her identity; her correspondence with
Breton bundled with his page proofs for *Nadja* and, in 2003,
catalogued and auctioned, kept in a private buyer's vault. But
also—thanks to the auction house of CalmelsCohen—as of
April 2003, temporarily drifting in hyperspace. I marvel at the
coincidence that Nadja's letters became accessible to me just as I
neared the completion of my work, my search for her, begun ten
years ago. I have been able to peer, sometimes of necessity through
a magnifying glass, at jpegs of lot 2119, the twenty-seven letters
Nadja wrote to André, pixels approximating the muted tones of
the envelopes, even the creases in them, the blots in the ink, the
increased pressure in the pen coinciding with the increased pressure
in the language. The voice that I had been imagining.

I've heard scientists on the fringes say life is only information, zeros
and ones linked in the line dance of eternity, in the mazes of alleys
where everyone is always meeting, every blind minute of the day.

The distances she crossed and the way time loops! For breathing
through us and giving us the slip. For the woman, irreducible, who

was more than ankles, wrists, the untended bit of ground outside
every grid—

I, Nadja

do solemnly swear, being of sound mind
and body, do swear, swear I
never loved you, you thief
of tongues, self-important *arriviste*
bastard. You entered me
like a café, proud of your mien, *très artiste.*
Already in that first moment I could see
the machines spinning in you,
the developer's eye that blurs
and distorts. So I lied to you.
I gave you something to work with,
your truth a cat's eye
narrowed to a slit. Too much light you said
scorches the casserole, was that it?
My scribbles dazzled, apparently.
But what you never cared to see, filaments
jutting out of me at the Perray-Vaucluse, those
would score your flesh.
I warn you, here, now, with my burning eyes
and my stained hands square on this table:
écoute André, je commence à faire entendre ma vérité.

Mad Money

When I wake up in the morning I splash cold water all over my face.
I eat nothing; what could be more mundane? I do not dress until
three—I like the smell of sleep to linger, hoping that dreams this way
will linger too. I make lists. Lists of apartments I've coveted, lists of
things to throw away or buy when I come across some money. My
mother told me always to have some mad money, for a rainy day,
she said. Only for unnecessary things, she said. But how am I to
distinguish? All my money is mad. It slips through my fingers as
though it grew scales. It throws itself from my windows, to swim
maniacally upstream. It starves itself into a state of grace. Erratic
as a 10 franc whore with swollen lips and a dog to feed.

Mercy on Our Poor Ambitious Souls

Chère Maman, you wonder what I can be doing in Paris. This question is your habitual postscript, your curiosity a shade beyond the pale. I wish I could say that I have made a name for myself already in the theatrical milieu. But let this suffice for the moment: I am staying at l'Hôtel du Théatre, rue de Cheroy. My room suits me well, with its artistic furniture, its Marquisette drapery. And its dark reed fern-stand transports me to our own parlour. So you are not so far away.

And I am not forlorn. These past two days have thrown sand in my engine though. I am waiting to hear about a part with some dancing. Will you forgive me Mother for my skewed priorities (how is my tzigane)? But then, this is why I came, what I am doing in Paris. Why be coy? I came, Maman, to inhabit the stage, I came to baptise myself under the burgundy curtain of the Theatre, to dip my slippers in the chalk trough stage left.

Well, this evening at any rate I am preparing for all this, the grit, the stars. But what can I do, more than I am? My hotel smells of Papier d'Arménie—rooms often occupied by ailing travellers. Let's be frank, I am among these. Let the Sovereign Lord have mercy on our poor ambitious souls. The doctor said my health is extremely delicate— those were his words—and that I should ship myself off to the Mont-Dore. This absurd thought gives me great pleasure as I daily wear a path in the sidewalk between here and the theatre district. I do not complain; it's my joy. I will not let this opportunity slip from me like the countless centimes that fell through the pocket of my old gabardine monstrosity of a coat!

I would be so glad if you sent a quilt, the faded apricot. Something to ward off the bone-aching damp that sits about in all the corners of my room when it rains.

I hope I see you soon, if God is willing, as Sister Dominique says,

Nadja —your Léona

Première Rencontre

I was crossing the Place Franz Liszt when,
through an open window above the florist's shop,

I heard someone playing Chopin,
and smiled at the irony. I stopped

because I had something stuck to my shoe.
He turned as I was about to pass,

and he held out his hands
like someone asking directions

or the salesgirl's advice on which scarf to select.
Was I supposed to swoon?

In one of his hands a book, wrapped in paper,
which I felt he wanted to unwrap for me.

In the other a question he needed me
to puzzle through.

We stood aside for someone to pass
and in that instant of moving closer to him

so as not to brush up against someone else, I knew
I could forget myself.

I had a hair appointment, it's true.
Just not that afternoon. His hand was warm.

We walked to a café, and sat
facing the entrance to the métro.

He will go home to his wife soon, no matter, I thought.
Although he hadn't said yet. The way he glanced

at his watch, it was that. Still, he was talking
and I began to feel the good chill

one feels after swimming all day with evening coming on
and autumn. I was talking rapidly.

For a few moments it was as if there were heavy curtains
around us, the world muffled. I looked at his face

for the first time then. When I picked up my glass
I had to use two hands.

I flicked my cigarette, the whole ember
split off. He was looking at my nails,

and then so did I.
What did I hope to happen?

He reminded me
of that young man I loved in Lille.

But even a glove on the street
can make you reach for it, thinking it's your own.

We Took the Train

on impulse to Saint-Germain-en-Laye, arriving very late
beside the Chateau, two blurred forms

by the curlicued railing, momentarily
transfixed by the shuddering lights of the city

the black box of the sky, the sleeping valley
we'd crossed to try to outrun this storm

even the gravel under my feet was singular
and, later, in the frayed light of our room

his low, monotonous, sleepy voice
his earlobe between my teeth, my lips

pressed kisses, my nose gently grazed
collarbone, knobs of the locked armoire of his heart

the bee buzzing in the nest of his throat—
the soft, deliberate way he said

I'm going to come now, I'm coming now
: now—

no more words, then
his throat a flower closing in the dark

Choreography for an Aubade

Lift her arms and look deep, long enough
to make us believe you see in her
the ecstatic flight of plastic pigeons
at Sacré Coeur:
temps levé, chassé passé,
brisé, yes!
Pause for the internal shudder
that makes a magazine slide off the lap, makes knives
clink against spoons in a steamship dining room. Now
let her see the softest smile your face knows

and she, she will kick the days since
along the sidewalk, old tin cans.

I had no little love for you. It spoke

beneath skin, whispered when you entered
rooms. The places you might fit into.

It has happened lately that I have held
every part of you. Impossible
to still them now, these hands. They sing
your shape through doorways, they sing
the whole house awake:

Some Shapes of Sadness

The shadow of a dying plant hanging in the corner of this room, a shade of grey only slightly paler than the shadow. Nothing moves and I am spending long hours fitting in. Not even wondering. Becoming inured to the way my stupid heart beats itself against my own grey wall. It is too tall an order to be loved.

I Close My Eyes

Each thing has its season, and beyond that the sweet dreams of oblivion, tra la. Little things like losing a favourite book, or noticing that a theatre I love has gone under break me in half. I spend the rest of the day in bed, flattening my head between two pillows. Loss a toxin in my blood.

During the idle hours, the fantasies! You're a star, dressed in a Chanel suit and alligator shoes. Stepping out of a chauffeur-driven Duesenberg. You are backlit and well rested. Cutting the sky in half with your proud hair. You drop something, and men knock heads trying to pick it up. Never mind, you threw it away.

Then it becomes clear that one of the men who couldn't even get close enough to knock heads with the others is the long lost one. You hardly noticed, you're so busy and important. You have someone to brush lint off your suit. But there isn't any lint on you, you never have to pluck hairs out of your own chin, your fingernails are slivers of moon in the pink air of Paris.

Oh Mon Feu, you say, like a lady stooping to pick up a lapdog. It's been so long. We should meet, at the old place. But you are being ushered along by your retinue, feathers from your boa swirling in your wake like sparks.

Chez Graff

André, I want my notebook, beef stew
that it is to you—to me it holds a certain
blue sky—my past life, fire and truth.
André, I want my notebook,

to shield my daughter, to pull the curtain
on my tangled life as an *ingénue*,
my dreams swept into the dustbin

the masks I shed for you
displayed on your study wall with pushpins.
Screw your game and your retinue,
André, I want my notebook!

My notebook,
the spine, the words, the drawings on onionskin—
I'm more than the specimen you
dissect in your book,

your limp-noodle vision of the feminine.
(You won't take off your shoes
at the beach!) I walk barefoot in the margins

of my notebook, naked and blue-
cold with the discipline.
You pursued me, and now I pursue you:
My notebook, André. My notebook.

Hairpin

1. Crimped

The curtain opens on Léona, still at home,
giving her blonde hair one hundred strokes.

Winter nights, in the dark of her attic room,
hunched over, beside her small daughter's palliasse,

she'd pull her boar's-bristle brush
from scalp to tips, emitting sparks

until her scalp was tingling, electrified,
the fly-aways a frail starburst, quivering

like the needle in an agitated compass.
Summer evenings, the lazy light

leaning in doorways, she'd remove kerchief and pins,
and then, with the yellow teeth of her cellulose comb,

the day's work: all her snarled strands, ends split,
snake-tongued, sun-bleached, a bit of straw, a bit of feather

from the goose she had helped her mother pluck.
And when her daughter jack-knifed from a dream,

Léona'd strike a match, the candle was lit *Here, see*
she'd sit on the edge of the bed, rubbing her wrists.

Look— (two hairpins, tucked under her nose,
the wires held there by her pursed lips: a crimped moustache

to make the kid laugh, drift back into sleep.) *Hush.*
The child's breath, the smouldering wick, the waxy air too close.

2. A dream featuring hairpins is an omen of happy future prospects.

Too close, the air, her daughter's sticky legs. Léona snags
on the nettles of sleep, clutching damp sheets

answering the telephone ringing in her mattress.
The hairs on her body piqued as antennae,

she starts awake, goes to the window, sees
the white-hot moon glide through the sky

quick as *sous* spilled from a pocket
slip down the sewer grate.

Gone. Before dawn
the door scrapes shut behind her, she bolts down the lane.

Think fire through parched grass—that frenzied pace.
Items shoved into her case: a monkey-skin felt hat, step-ins

and cotton drawers, a dress with turn-back cuffs, hose,
an overblouse in reseda green, hairpins,

Mer Dentifrice, Madame Hélène's Vanishing Creme.
Too much, not enough. Maybe they'd be relieved she left

behind her one good mistake. And then there was the company
she kept! Staying out late, coming home bruised.

Random connections she snatched out of the air like seedclocks
and blew back into the air, fingers winnowing the unseen wake.

When the cock crowed, Maman read the note
Léona'd stuck to yesterday's loaf with a hairpin.

Not to weigh down one's thoughts with the weight of one's shoes
she walked barefoot to Lille by fields of lady's tresses, twayblades.

Walked through the Place du Théatre before boarding the train
at the Gare du Lille. A one-way ticket to Paris, a new name.

3. Bending the Truth, Première Rencontre

I'm on my way to a hairdresser
        on the Boulevard Magenta, she says,
palm smoothing the flurry of hair
at the nape of her neck,
        eyes flitting like a leaf in traffic.

        Well, in that case… His fingers
brush her temple pursuing an errant pin. His
tongue hairpins in his mouth.
        Votre épingle de cheveux, Mademoiselle:

        And she reaches for it then
perching in his fingers like a butterfly.

4. *Inexorable Machines*

Several times Nadja drew Breton with his hair standing on end
—as though sucked up by a high wind—like long flames.

Did she see her own devouring element in him,
the shivering and twisted filaments linking them

as the pistons and pendulums in Picabia's erotic machines,
made so that they cannot work, the wonder

and the failure automatic?

5. Undone

In the Sainte-Anne they took away her hairpins
plucked *sit still, silly goose* from her whirlwind hair. One

patient there swallowed hairpins, among other things.
So they looked under Nadja's tongue. They looked

in other cavities, her wiry limbs held down
by orderlies, legs pulled apart, pinned.

Afterwards she doubled over
sobbing her daughter's name.

6. Riddle, a Found Poem

Long legs, crooked
thighs, no head
and no eyes

Waiter, Café de la Régence

Comes in most days now.
Dolled up she was, at first,
when Monsieur was coming in regularly
for his *cinq à sept*.

She orders, and sits for hours
stroking her gloves like a spaniel
or clenching her fists
between bouts of scribbling
on the café stationery.

Lately she crumples
and rewrites page after page.
So I told her two sheets is the limit,
after that she could look to G. Lalo.
She should ease up a bit,

show some decorum.
Yesterday she begged a cigarette.
Fingers too shaky to roll one of her own.
And a hole in her stockings.
Didn't even bother with the gloves.
I don't know, I guess

because it was raining, because she was
drenched, I set before her a café crème,
put the stationery under the counter
and wiped down the espresso machine
for the second time. Couldn't look at her.

Here again today! Chérie,
the writing's on the wall. Your friend
is dipping his pen elsewhere.

Cutting Time

This hour is shaped
                   like a gall stone.
Did you want to go alone
through the slush, leaving me to think
how your hat sucks
your unruly head like a lime.
When Chagall was born
they thought he had 2 hearts. Sure,
until they cut him open
and a wild eye of a horse
blinked magical ooze
over sterile white tiles. O
spasms of ablated colour. O aureate tear.   Maybe

just now a sheaf of your ripe hair
is winnowing through slender fingers,
growing a splendid Alberta at your feet.

Against Longing

You will dazzle me no more. I will
not open drawers to find small things you gave me
in that other life.
No dreams, *Smooth Neck*, do not
whisper to me at the poetry stacks, in the bath —
You have had too much of me.
Now is to feel the sidewalk, the tea towel,
the cabbage, the tears.

My Friend,

Are you still at the Henri IV?
I hope this letter finds you.

When I asked for your help before, a few francs
to get me out of that fix, I couldn't have known

I would be prevented from meeting you
at our little table in the Place Dauphine.

And now I don't know what to do, I'm lost.
I have only one shoe! Slippers

the nurse gave me. I was brought here
two days ago. Nurse is writing this.

My heart paces its cage, paces,
there is nowhere to go.

M. Breton has deserted me.
If you could manage to come here,

it would help—
more than the money, which I was so desperate for.

I know I said it bothered me
but you can call me Lena. It would be fine,

I would know you were talking
to someone you loved.

Forecast: Nadja

I knew everything, so hard have I tried to read in my streams of tears.
    — Nadja

The essential thing is that I do not suppose there can be much
difference for Nadja between the inside of a sanitarium and the
outside.
    —André Breton, *Nadja*

Flowers drown when the ground gets sodden.
I knew everything, so hard have I tried
to notice things,
to read in my streams of tears.

I knew everything, so hard.
Fingers thrumming, nails chewed down,
I tried to read in my streams of tears
the prognosis, the weather report. More rain:

fingers thrumming, nails. Down
water and pills.
The prognosis, the weather report? More rain
apparently. That's what I can expect:

water and pills.
Storm clouds drop like a dressing gown.
Apparently, that's what I can expect.
And then after a time the weather clears.

Storm clouds drop like a dressing gown
again. Months later I visit the garden.
For a time, the weather's clear.
So delicate I scarcely touch the ground.

Again, months later, I visit the garden:
mayflies braid the air

so delicate I scarcely touch the ground,
like girls skipping Double Dutch,

mayflies braiding the air.
And for now I feel good in my skin
like girls skipping Double Dutch
one, two, beside my slatted wood bench.

And for now I feel good in my skin.
The girls are singing
three, four, beside my slatted wood bench
something luminous, the beginning of the word hope.

The girls are singing,
Rain, rain, go away, come again another day, and
something luminous, the beginning of the word hope
is folded with their skipping ropes.

Rain's come again, rain another day.
At the Sainte-Anne, I'm put away.
Hopes furl like the skipping ropes,
like umbrellas in the lost and found.

At the Sainte-Anne, I'm put away.
Who could distinguish me from the other
umbrellas in the lost and found?
The nurses kindly take me out for air.

Who could distinguish me from the others
shuffling along the tree-lined Allée Paul Verlaine,
inmates the kindly nurses take outside for the air
darkening slatted benches under the linden trees?

Lines from Verlaine I've always loved
repeat my pain, like the rain
darkening slatted benches under the linden trees:
il pleure dans mon cœur comme il pleut sur la ville.

The rain repeats my pain, like
the grating sound of a key turning in a lock.
O bruit doux de la pluie par terre et sur les toits!
In a week I'm moved to the Perray-Vaucluse.

The grating sound of a key turning in a lock,
the wretched view of the garden—
the week I'm moved to the Vaucluse
I begin to know everything.

The wretched view of the garden.
The stone wall, gatehouse, regimen.
I begin to know everything:
the difference between the inside of a sanatorium

and the outside of a sanatorium.
When I'm clear they let me stroll the grounds.
When I'm threatening rain, they lock me in again.
Somebody turns the water on and off.

When I'm clear they let me stroll the grounds
to notice things. Long walks in the rain make me
so muddy the bath water turns brown.
Flowers drown.

Button Up Your Overcoat

More beauty than you or I can bear.
Yesterday Louis and I rode the train
down to Epinay-sur-Ørge
to see how she is faring, your Nadja.

Clouds hung black and low
over the hospital, very theatrical.
We chose not to read this as a sign.

We missed the worst of it:
the rain came down in sheets
once we were inside
scraping some chairs together.

A nurse brought Nadja
a pill to take; she made a weak joke
about invisible friends.
Indeed, we all did our best
to keep it light.

Didn't ask about you.

The acuity of her loss, though—I knew
a cleaner version of it
after Gala left me
for the moustache
and everyone took me for dead.

Granted I see why you consider it best
to button up your overcoat
and keep dark as far as she is concerned.
The sphinx is thin and cage-chafed
as the lions in the menagerie.

Frankly, she's not going anywhere soon.
You thought she was delicate before.

Her nerves are shot. Shot.
Smoking one of my cigarettes
she looked like a mouse drinking from a spout.

Sugared Violets

You brought me sugared violets,
set the package from *A La Mère de Famille*
on the bedside table, next to a glass of stale water.
"Something instead of the pills," you offered

the flower of unrequited love, clipped
and frozen in its longing
like Mallory climbing to the indigo crest
of Everest, heart

lurching in that direction
well into the next century.
We are made of dust.
We clutch at the object of our desire,

we slip. From below we see the way
light hits cheekbone, summit, moon.
You brought me sugared violets, you're gone
from my sick room.

Bruised chrysalis on my tongue
dissolves, blooms.

The Slenderness of Forgetting

Louis* has come, and Eugène** with him.
But you, never, God spit! You who took the train with me,
and unfolded yourself like yesterday's newspaper.
Who closed the window to hear my baroque laugh
you said in all its detail. And now she drags her shame
around like an IV they must have muttered, crossing
that wet lip of lawn back to the station.

No, I must say it—even as my bones are crumbling and my body
has developed a sordid counterplot of its own: you
who have sold me, and for what?
To repay the few paltry francs slipped into my hand?

In point of fact, this turns that brutal sailor's fist into a flower:
nasturtium, yes, even palatable. And you wept at *that*!
I would give you that blackened eye and that split lip—
three square meals a day, stash some of it
in your sock drawer, press it in the pages of your Trotsky.
My scars for you, because I have only them now.

And, oh yes, my envying. Envying in you always
the slenderness of forgetting

* Aragon
** Paul Eluard, pseudonym of Eugène Grindel

Dear Mademoiselle Nadja

I write to you because we have mutual friends, Paul Eluard and Louis
    Aragon,
who have told me about your situation and—without having to say very
    much—

imparted to me the sense that you might be glad to receive a letter. Now
I know this is not the letter you (or anyone) might hope for. As I said

we have mutual friends, as well as (I hope you will forgive me) a mutual
    antagonist
in Monsieur Breton. But I do not write to commiserate with you on that
    subject—though,

by his own account, he might have spurred your crisis by spurning your
    affections.
I do commiserate with you on this (not unrelated) matter:

I too was convalescing, a couple of years ago (about a year after my first
    encounters
with the surrealists) and desperate for correspondence, which I found to
    be in short supply.

(Mine was a mental and nervous crisis of limited proportions, but
    enough
to quite incapacitate me for a time. I recovered in the Cévennes.)

It's too bad you and I just missed crossing paths: when you were
    admitted by André
to his circle, I was just spinning out of it. But for that we might have run
    into one another

at the Gallery in the Rue Jacques Callot.
Like Breton, I'm attracted to the individual, a live wire.

He collects them like African masks and *objets d'art*. I feel
amply rewarded to have ridden a current with them for a while.

These last sentences were tedious to write, and no doubt to read as well.
I want to say simply that you needn't fear: while I do not abhor the hyena
      and the vulture,

I bear no affinity with these creatures. As for the lion—let him roam!
I write solely in the hope of bringing cheer with this azure ink

on paper of a certain weight, folded into a lined envelope, and sealed
      with wax,
such as you were perhaps used to receiving. And which soon will be
      carried to you

and put into your hand. If it is a good day, and I hope it is, I imagine
      that
you might be sitting on a bench beneath one of the shady trees facing the
      creek

and (beyond that) the train station at Epinay-sur-Ørge. And that you
      may soon be home.

—Francis Ponge, June 1928

Pay as you go

Grief comes in installments,
a small package each season
so you can afford it. When it comes
hold it up as a light catcher
to imploded windows, crawl
        into its tremulous utricle
to lose your sense of balance, to know
your centre of gravity. Study
the awful chrestomathy, the corners
of rooms, the ash
        in your coffee, the heft
                        of things dropped
        Accidents
happen.

Afterwards sleep,
a Fabergé egg.

Send it back, and you may
have nothing at all, or worse
a stomach full of stone mouths
when the world throws up its hands.

Ten

My daughter is ten years old today. My mother brought her to Armentières to visit. She wore a dress with pansies embroidered on the collar. Green ribbons in her hair. She gave me a loose hug and turned her cheek for me to kiss, and then she sat on her hands, kicking her feet, which still dangle several inches above the floor. When Maman's hand came down softly on her knee to still her fidgeting, she leaned into her like a cat rubbing against the kitchen door.

I tell her that at this asylum there was once a blind boy who could calculate quick as skin the solution to any mathematical problem. Square roots. The day of the week corresponding to a given date. How many seconds someone of a certain age had been alive. "You're ten, how many seconds is that? A million?"

"Why was he here, because he was blind?"

"As a youth he pretended to be mad to escape from somewhere worse, and they kept him here until he was grown up. Then he toured Paris and England, solving math problems in a tuxedo."

"When will they let you out?" Lou-Lou asked, playing with her braids.

"I am working on my arithmetic. What's ten times ten?"

Out came her hands and her fingers opened like flowers, her toes pointing to the ceiling.

Twelve Years Later

I see the date of our first meeting

in the corner of a paper forgotten

and down

        you fall again

like a jar

of preserves

from a crammed cupboard.

                    What a mess.

Later I see someone has closed this drawer
of winter things, leaving
the fingers of a scarf
bleeding outside.

October 12, 1938.

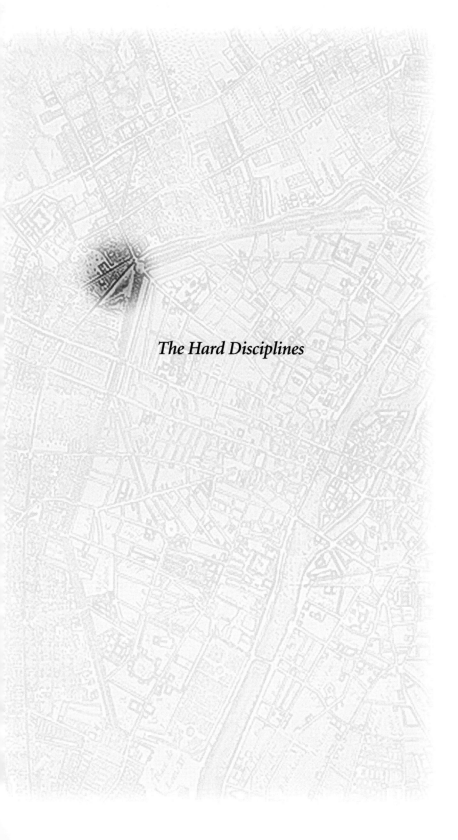

The Hard Disciplines

1. Geometry Lesson

Sitting oblique as perfection on the parallel bars,
I was minding my nephew in the park.

You could smell cut grass, hear
someone pushing a lawn mower, making it summer.

It was dusk,
I still had trust.

So I answered the teenager on the ten-speed
who stopped to get directions and stayed to teeter,

his thick fist gripping one of the bars below.
When answers began to amount to

a conversation, I tried to shrink
from the fraught intersection—

concentrating on my nephew toddling nearby
to show I wasn't flattered by

his lingering, honeyed words about my hair.
I lowered myself from the parallel bars

and the strange boy bulked, suddenly magnified.
He dropped the bike, its muddy back tire

spinning. The mower started up again behind the fence,
and I turned to clutch my nephew. Percipience?

How could I bend, extend my arms
in the radius of so much harm?

He jumped me from behind,
climbed me like a tree, willowed my spine,

my neck in the triangle of his left arm—
headlocked—he threw his right arm

over my shoulder and ploughed his hand
between my legs like a dog digging in the sand.

You're so beautiful, he whined into my ear.
A voice inside me said *You are here*—

the endpoint: scrubbing myself red
in a scalding shower or bravely splayed for the rape kit

my sister's kid searching my face
a form on the ground traced by police.

Suddenly my twig of an arm snapped back,
my bud of a fist gave his nose a crack,

and then my elbow doubled him up, to show him
what angles a girl can devise. Full of adrenaline,

I grabbed my reeling nephew and made a break for it,
overturning every simple theory in the world.

2. Physics: After the Genesis Concert, 1982

My bedroom measured say 10' by 12'.
Momentum equals mass times velocity,
and what did I weigh, 95 lbs? Skinny.
One door, one window, one bed, flowered sheets.
I'd closed the drapes, was naked, half-asleep,
conch-eared, buzzed on blow-over weed. *Psst.*
I jolted awake: *Who's there?* Stroking his need,
he leaned in the doorway to my room. *A seat?*
he begged, gesturing to my pink bedspread.
He was sizing me up, my brother's friend.
One door, and he blocked it. Forget what you've read
about sailing, tacking into the wind —
I resolved this force with words:
                    Go ahead
and when he moved I shot past him, a warhead.

3. Algebra

from the Arabic al-jabr, *reunion of broken parts*

Let us for a moment say we need
to work on the rational and radical expressions of our need.

Let one side be y
and the other y,

to open the question, redintegrate
the vulgar fraction of one above the other—

where the power imbalance starts.
Let us learn this algebra, reunion of broken parts.

4. Calculus

from the Latin for small stone, used in reckoning on an abacus

This one fought until her neck snapped like a chain.
This one gave in and was strangled anyway.
This one was kept four years in a hole.
Another tried to observe the generalized power
rule: stay stone still, think *dead*, be small—
and hold her breath into infinity.

The symbol for infinity
is a detached link of a broken chain,
a dead girl with hips and breasts, small.
God help me, I'm small. Powerless
to protect my daughter, keep her whole.

I can form a precious chain
of words slighter than the number of girls killed this year.

Supposing I had real power,
to quicken a chain of girls curving into infinity.

5. Statistics

If a story is not to be about love, then I think it must be about fear.
—Diane Schoemperlen, "The Look of the Lightning, the Sound of the Birds."

You've heard the statistics.
Like dark matter, they clot the imagination,
every now and then make you ball
up in grandmother's afghan, a tub of melting
ice cream on the arm of the couch. Afraid
to be touched.
>   *One or two women per week are killed*
>   *by a spouse or ex-spouse, boyfriend or ex-boyfriend.*
It's too much.
Some days you can't leave the house.
You cancel the paper, petition
the chain letter gods: Inoculate us
against random tragedies.
And give us something stronger than flannel
for the not-so-random ones. *Two-thirds*
of sexual assaults occur in a private home.
You've got to get out more. Go to the beach.
It's summer, eat fries smothered in malt vinegar
on a concrete bench beside the concession stand. *Each year*
there is one ton of cement poured for each man, woman and child
in the world. This does not mean that your passing, accidental
premature or eventual will mean one ton less.

You're getting old. Now in reverse
making invisible
notches on the door frame.
From the age of thirty,
humans gradually begin to shrink in size. Something you realized
when you were five, passengering in the back seat
while your Dad drove. Safely buckled in,
sweaty knees sticking to the vinyl. Before
there were shoulder straps in the back. A rear-ender

and you'd have been folded like a bobby pin
for life. Scratch

your hives, decompress, forgive
your facial twitch with a cold cloth. We wish
we could be of more assistance. But
that's not really our department.
Try Philosophy or Religious Studies; they deal
with the why side of things.
In the meantime, fill out this form,
complete this survey, stick it
in the tray by the door. Leave
a number if you're willing
to be contacted.
            According to ancient Chinese astrologers,
                70% of omens are bad.
Still so many calculations to be made.
An anodyne? Sit back under this two-bit moon, little numberling,
take comfort in this reckoning: *In a lifetime*
we replace our skins approximately one thousand times.

6. Chemistry

for Wes Folkerth

and to the finer chemistries
that make up, and renew him,
every seven years, exactly
as he is, affirming everything.

Change of Heart   *Bronwen Wallace*

This year makes six since we cossed over, into
marriage, this ordinary brownstone, this house
made of hummingbirds. Seven, since we first
touched palms, ignited, lived close to the flame.
That we've managed to stay there, warm, sane,
neither of us succumbing to disease,
seven year itch, the lure or curse of statistics,
stills me. When he returns from this long journey,
we'll raise a glass to new discoveries
and to the finer chemistries

that kept us, keep us, coming back for more:
the sublime stitching of energy and mass
the distant tungsten burners of the night
witness and bless; the perfect resonance
of two complex structures, ours.
More than once, fully awake (the twin
engines of our cats in the duvet clouds
around us), I've studied the poetry of
the cells, elements—carbon, oxygen . . .
—that make up, and renew him,

this man who was born. Who breathes beside me
every night. Basic elements, standard
measurements. Beyond this, he cannot be glossed.
What makes us who we are, all shoulder or art?
How do we learn to love what we need?
Not volatile, stable. Gentle symmetry.
Wonderingly, we're content to watch the light

show of unresolvable substances
repeating their elemental glory
every seven years, exactly.

My first lover tried to choke me. Seven
years we were together, and for seven years
after leaving him I smoked like a chimney;
took that part with me. Dark
alchemy. I transmuted what pain still lived.
Maybe love is the hardest discipline.
Simplest formula, arcane catalyst—
who can name all its allotropes?
This climacteric I'm remade, glittering
as he is, affirming everything.

7. Geography: Long Winter, 45° N 73° W

By February it's like going to the orthodontist's,
squirming in the vinyl chair,
wincing with each adjustment *just a little*
more here, a little more.
So many tiny elastics about to snap.
Mouths clamped open in a Munchian scream.
Sick of staring at the same stained ceiling.
Enough!
we want to see tulips instead,
and crocuses clawing their way out of the dirt. Oh!
to wear a T-shirt, mules and mini-skirt,
leave the damn headgear at home.

Some of us stumbled out again today, still numb.
You who were with me in the waiting room, do you see?
Water is sheeting crossways over sidewalks into gutter streams.
Let this be the Great Gargle and Rinse.
When the braces finally come off, when
these concrete pearly whites smile us, perfectly, into May.

8 April, 2001

8. Biology: Going to Seed

Seems cruel and unnatural, this cutting
back before the flower blooms. Though indeed
necessary. My mother's atrophied
for lack of it, I guess. She's muttering
about her messy life, finds balancing
difficult, tangled in her own deep weeds.
Can pruning save us all from going to seed?
At thirty I shrink from this hard gardening.
Dad, on the other hand, cut way back, near
to the roots: threw out his old suits, cars, kids,
wife, got himself a lush new life, flourished
dandelion-hardy, apparently, those years
before the disease took hold. He forbids
us to plant him in the ground, fold his veined wrists.

Give my body to science, Dad insists,
leaving us wondering how he'll be dispersed,
circle this cold earth, a milkweed husk burst
open. Cross-sectioned for pathologists
researching myasthenia gravis.
Stunted, doddering, his knurled body thirsts
now for expanding his cramped universe,
as the cucumber or clematis twists,
unravelling traveller's joy and other spry creepers
pull themselves clear out of the cold frame.
He's talked of taking up the motorcycle
instead of the electric wheelchair. We fear
he'd speed, swerve, scatter himself like grain.
He'll have no grave. Says: plant elder, honeysuckle.

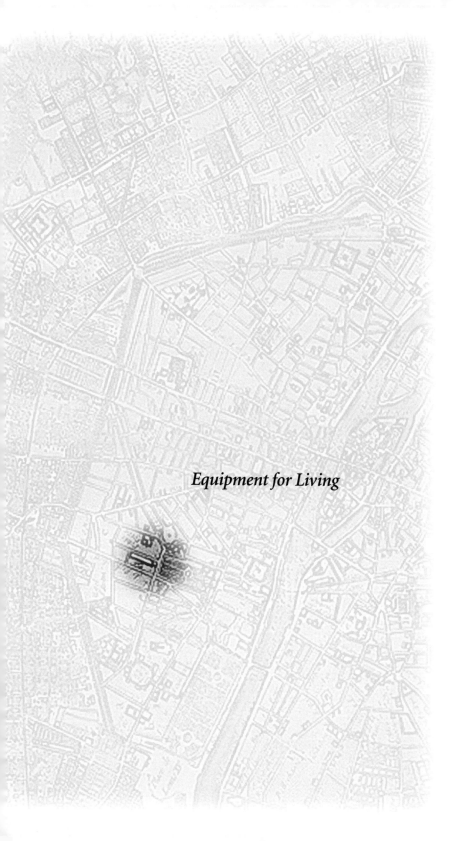

Equipment for Living

Accessories After the Fact

Prudish chaperone of décolletage,
scarf muffles a multitude of sins:
hides a hickey, stray nips and tucks,
scratch marks that gloss
the lady-killer's lost hours.

Belt is used to wallop the children
and to hold up Papa's pants —
grants the prisoner a quick escape,
finds loopholes.

Bag, what are you hiding in there?
If they could only find the bag of bloody clothes.

Gloves. Need I say more?

Keep it under your hat.

Glance at watch too much
and it gets itchy, time's wheelman
puts the pedal to the metal
and you're hung out to dry.
Builds your trust and then clocks you:
the rendezvous missed,
the life. Tick tick tick
of your own scapegoat heart.

Dark shades cover a shiner, cliché
the bad cop in his mirrored tear drops.

Shoes will carry you from one misdeed to another.
You wear them out, dragging them along
on sordid errands,
in the summer wet with dew,
in the winter stinging with salt —
when you take them off they cringe.

Towards a Study of the Trench Coat

First Impressions

The trench coat is the Tablewater Biscuit of outerwear. When
it is working it forgets you can smile. Such humble roots in the
trenches of W.W.I, but look at it now, what a social climber!
Protecting some of the smartest suits around: Morley Safer,
American Anchorman, admits to owning five, a small army.
Rain, sleet, and (throw in a lining) snow assault its panels and
seams, and fall at its hem. Wonderful, but can it do for the
politician ducking a cream pie what chain-mail once did for
knights dodging arrows? The trench coat will not save you
from drowning in sorrows.

At least it's not a fair-weather friend; it's there when you need
it, unlike the umbrella that gave you the slip at the deli, turning
inside out, tumble-weeding along the sidewalk, speaking the
language of November leaves.

London Fog

the skin of an angel
in St. James's Park

the soft and near perfume
of damp sleeves in the Tube

your voice a whisper
in the hiss of closing doors

the slapdash kiss of trench coat
brushes my leg — oh

dear, oh dear, you are everywhere

Imperméable

All business, nondescript,
it promises the same cachet
to the man operating incognito
and the lady executive
storming the glass ceiling.

You bought one yourself
and one for your lover. A private joke
between you: the uniform
of clandestine meetings, taupe
bland as your sex lives at home.

There you are waiting on the platform,
risking a perfunctory kiss. You sense a chill
in those lips? Or has your own desire
lost its edge, become as understated
as the coat on your back?

With a thumbnail you scratch
out last spring's mustard stain, and
hear a salamander scampering
across a cool tile floor, echoing
your need for more fluid escapes.

Suitable for saying goodbye, pockets perfect
for carrying someone else's train ticket,
retreating,
            that tight-lipped slit of a mouth
doesn't tell you anything.

Architectural Chairs

for Marion Quednau

It could be said that when we design a chair, we make a society and
city in miniature. Certainly this has never been more true than in this
century [...]. It is not an exaggeration to say that the Miesian city is
implicit in the 'Mies' chair.

— Peter Smithson, British Architect

Lady Armchair, 1951
(designer: Marco Zanuso)

Half lounge chair, half
tank; in moss-coloured velvet and stilettos
she manoeuvres through the doorway
to your den or home studio
and the occupation begins. That performance
that somehow ended up on the cutting-room floor.
Camera, action! Close up:
she drags on a cigarette, removes a bracelet,
uncrosses, re-crosses her gleaming legs,
a shoe dangling from the toes of her polished foot
stirring the air like a dynamo.
Cut.
In another scene
she'll carry her tumbler in one hand and those shoes
in the other, traipse through the garden
to your patio door, needing
ice. Many times
you'll rehearse the same lines.
She's got ideas, never mind
armrests like the flanks of an Italian starlet
fed on ricotta, olive oil, melon.
Shorn and love-sleek, she's ripe ripe ripe.
Why should we not be comfortable, darling?
It's so boring here.

Lifetimes after the casting couch, she is
the director's wife, the life of the party.
A martini followed by a long massage?
A little pumice for the soul, you dirty, dirty.
Come to Mama.
Whoever sinks into me
is swallowed whole
and aches to be forgotten.

Ox Chair and Ottoman, 1960
(designer: Hans J. Wegner)

You don't have to be Texan
to want one.
In leather, black
as a doctor's bag
full of cool steel instruments,
smoother than a Mexican saddle,
with a footrest like a lolling sun-
blackened tongue.
The silhouette: a super-sized keyhole
through which you squint
at everything char-
everything brandable.
No bucking bull here. Dull
as conversation between men who clean
guns for fun. But dark as oil,
as high noon, the saloon
door swinging, the perverse pleasure
of watching one black hat
force another to dance.

How many removes is that?
A fantasy of a fantasy
of the loner versus the herd,
of rest after back-breaking work,
of (let's admit it) the Wild Wild
domesticated. Bad guys who come home
with the cows, hang
up their holsters, finally
settle down.
Into furniture, the ultra-
domesticated animal.
Can we bottle this?
Upholster it? Eureka!

> Meanwhile, back at the ranch-
> house (open-concept, indoor pool)

we're barbecuing
marinated sirloin
and baby back ribs, smothering
cob-corn in butter and crushed black pepper.
Crack open a cold one.
Take a load off.
Like all good beasts of burden
I have learned, who helps you
helps himself.

Barcelona Lounge Chair
(designer: Ludwig Mies van der Rohe)

Always smug in the pages of *Architectural Digest*. In pairs,
in uniform black and chrome,
squaring off with the pale sofa.

                                     Ahem.

They police the living room,
holding out their open briefcases.

                                     Pay up:

      ornament is a crime.
      Do we need to spell it out for you?
      You've become sloppy and you're too fat.
      Lose a few pounds
      as well as those cushions. Chintz!
      Cowhide or fur is acceptable, but barely.
      And buttons must be covered
      in the same material and used sparingly.
      You should feel them. None of this princess and pea
      shit. Everything is overstuffed,
      I'm queasy—You queasy?
      Turn down the heat in here, you could fry
      an egg on that chandelier. And what, precisely,
      is the function of this bric-a-brac?

The sofa reaches for its wallet,
the side chair searches through the roll-top desk
for its papers.

                    OK

      pedigreed Windsor, you can stay. Though old
      and flawed by unnecessary curves,
      some Windsors live in Mies's own house.

A murder of crows, an unkindness of ravens.
I call a showroom of these glossy black birds
a Gestapo of Barcelonas. Perhaps that's not fair;
I love this chair. Who doesn't

love it like discipline and spring
cleaning—the kind of toil that's hard
until you are done
and then step back. Yes,
just as it should be. Perfection.

Chaise Longue: Six Angles
(designer: Le Corbusier, Charlotte Perriand and Pierre
Jeanneret, 1928)

1.

Everything unnecessary stripped away
like a Band-Aid from a wound—that raw

that clean.

2.

A cross between a hammock and a dentist's chair;
whether you can relax in it depends on the angle

of your vision.

3.

A surreal x-ray of the tooth you'd take the pliers to:
the bleak topography of

a black cavity
stretched and bolted to the roots of a molar.

Notice the chipped enamel. Brace yourself.
Response to the technological sublime

is visceral and cerebral, originates
in the spine.

4.

get in
recline; inflect
your body's verb, float
foetal
in this anti-gravity machine, sling
and splint
for the modern
sickness (whatever
it is) this is
furniture as opiate

5.

We collaborate to discover our threshold of pain, the heights
of our ceilings. The architects give us equipment for living:

a severely reduced version of recliner
with all of its structure and operations revealed.

Because there's nothing like dishonesty in furniture
to keep us awake at night, to interfere

with the work of our hands,
the great sweep and delicate surgeries of daily life

the various poses and articulations of history

6.

When she conceived of the incline of the moveable component,
Charlotte Perriand had in mind a soldier at rest under a tree

free, presumably,
of injuries as well as minor discomforts

such as cold;
the pillow recalls a blanket rolled

to support a standard-issue neck and head
on the conveyor belt of dreams

The New Apartment

for Wes, who moved us in, and made it fit for habitation

It is hungry for our love
and waiting to be coaxed back.

The last tenants' dog left
flaps of his coat
in every corner, the musty smell
of resentment at having to sleep
in the basement, and dust
kicked up by his paws
chasing the forty grey squirrels
in the park of his dreams
nosed into the floorboards
along with his drool.

We inherit, as well, the original
1920s kitchen cupboards, wood
porous as coral, and sour
with the work of hands,
with garlic and grease.
And between the bathroom and hallway, a sun well
choked with dirt from a potted plant
that split its girdle;
seasons of leaves
dropped like snotty hankies.

I'm grateful for the saving graces:
bleach, paint, and habituation.
The double-bassist who practices downstairs.
Another kind of devotion.
This winter we'll practice
huddling by the hearth, watching sparks
centipede up the chimney as the wind
takes another deep haul. Outside,

the houses fat as linebackers
put on shoulder pads, helmets of snow,
get ready for the big pile-up.
Under so many layers
we'll forget we were ever unborn
ever unhoused.

Housewarming Song

(written at Hawthornden Castle Retreat for Writers, Scotland)

Tonight I sat at my desk and sketched
  the rooms of the house we will live in
    together, when I return to Montreal. To marry

    our furniture to the naked floors, earnest linoleum,
  warm baseboards. Wondering what will thrive
behind French doors, on slender balconies

in summer: a potted lemon tree, lavender, Sweet William. Imagine
  the chairs' shoulders warmed by the light
    from the sun well. Our raft of a bed

    drifting on a Sunday morning.
  I've been away from home, from your hands, for so long.
Away from domestic tasks and pleasures

to write uncertain things down.
  A bird scratches its song on the sky.
    The logs in the fireplace are damp and complaining.

    Each day I build a fire, and turn over the cinders.
  Jot things down, like
my body is the house your hands are remembering.

Unless These Notes

At her desk in the corner the music teacher is marking.
A mug full of red pencils. A stack of exercise books.
Somewhere beyond this: vacation.

A child has stayed after school. She enters the room,
a winter-thin animal approaching a village.
She has composed a song, wants to play it

for the teacher. She explains
it's about the wish for spring to come, and holding
the brown recorder like a flower in both hands,

takes a breath.
Dirty fingernails rise and fall
over the nostrils of the recorder.

Notes like crumbs on a kitchen table.
A baby crying in the apartment across the hall,
reedy and green. In the lemony light

the child dips over half a piece of lined paper,
marks on a staff, a scrolled treble clef.
Her hair needs washing.

Song's done. Unless these notes
follow us across the patchy field, melting the snow
clinging hard to the ditches and sunless balconies.

Vancouver Collection

Spring arrives with the hosing off of porches.
Men move from garages to mud rooms
with nails in their mouths.
Children's coats are open, mothers
squint into the sun, staying longer than yesterday.
The mountains plum, tulip-moist and plush.

And yet, at the intersection, you are
reminded of last winter's emblem: a crow
in the middle of the wet street, piercing
open a package of dog food, waiting
for tires to crow-size the stony kernels.

You came to Vancouver to slough off old skin. To re-begin
you left many things behind: the sturdy furniture, almost all
your books, your cobbled French, scuffed
floors and the salt on your boots. To indulge the yearning
to be at ease in your own language

you passed a summer glossy
as the leaves on the towering laurel hedges
dividing your place from the co-op.
You'd stand there with your harnessed cat
while he chewed on grass, front row centre in the green theatre.
A huge spider spun out its web. Summer progressed
through several acts; you were entertained:
the cucumber flowering, the tomato blushing,
holes in the laurel leaves
making the caterpillars plump, the deck growing mossy.
The only drama: the cat pounced on a wasp;
his pill-box foot fat as a key-chain catcher's mitt.

But a winter of heavy rain and stoned neighbours,
poor insulation, the unpredictable chill
of strangers, hearing for the first time in years
your own language stale, delivered

as lines from a second-rate movie, sometimes
empty, inane as the names of furniture stores—
Suite Dreams, Knock on Wood,
Once Upon a Tree, Pine Addictions—
tired you out. Curtain.

No wonder you are collecting again.
Assembling things about you that give
shape to the pang of not belonging.
Bowls, containers, baskets, anything empty:
the hollow sound of drums, tole egg, shallow pannier, rough
chipped canisters of enamelled tin, kettle, cruet, vial, tray,
pail, cup, reticule, retort. Things
with veneer, shell, paint;
things vesicular, lacquered
things with cracks.

Next, empty crates to take this cargo
back home to Montreal. Moving vans.
That hungry crow, your own bowed ribs.

Ex Libris

for Michael Bristol

Learning is weightless.

The day you dropped ballast
in the hallway outside your office
word spread quickly.
Folks plumbed those cardboard boxes, avid
for knowledge? real estate? Whatever;
they were lugging the stuff away.
Relieving you
of what I imagine lately amounted to
a tangle of garden hoses in your tool shed:

So many words.
Tomes and monographs,
paperbacks, hardbacks.
Each straight spine
a silent reprimand
a sulky, brittle friend, turning
away: dog-eared and pressing leaves
from autumns past; review
copy; desk copy; gift?
inscribed; full of notes
in the margins; pages
still uncut.
Shelves and shoulders starting to bow
with the weight
of too long since and may never yet.

In this scene you are facing down your shelves,
seeing the gain in the loss: every time
you squeeze a section of books
like a bandoneon between two palms
and da da dum da da dump them
into the box, you feel slightly freer.
Dust unsettled by your exertion

reels in the air. Space
to think.
The corners of the room munificent.

Let others amass and display
like the Grand Vizier of Persia
who, 10 centuries ago, had 117 000 volumes
carried wherever he went by 400 camels
trained to walk in alphabetical order.
Into the box.

Along McGill College Avenue last summer
there was a photography exhibit. You see it,
that one amazing aerial view
of a caravan crossing a desert?
At first you couldn't really see the camels
or the heavy loads they carried.
You saw their *shadows*

their forms in italics
transcribing the copious sands
with one of the unused words for wonder.

A Note about the Cover Image

I came across the image that Alan Siu has framed and incorporated into the book's cover design during my research trip to Paris (funded by a Canada Council grant), in April, 2001. I was there to retrace the steps of Breton and Nadja. Because their first meeting was of great importance to Breton, I started by looking for the exact spot where it had happened. He indicates in *Nadja* that the meeting occurred late in the afternoon on the Rue Lafayette, but (despite his apparent interest in facts) he does not know the name of the intersection he crossed just before seeing the young woman. He does mention that it was in front of a church, and that he had come from the *Humanité* bookstore. Visible above an awning in Breton's photograph of the bookstore is the number 120, which I surmised was the address. So by piecing together some of the details and literally retracing his steps along the Rue Lafayette in the 10th district, I was able to determine that the intersection was Place Franz Liszt, and the church he referred to was l'Eglise St. Vincent de Paul.

I spent my last full day in Paris, a Sunday, at the Saint-Ouen Flea Market (Breton's regular haunt of a Sunday). Rummaging through one of the postcard stalls, looking for images of the 10th district, I found this postcard from the mid-nineteen-twenties: a woman standing two steps from where Nadja and Breton first met.

Acknowledgements and Notes

Some of these poems have been previously published (sometimes in different versions) in the following publications: *In Fine Form: The Anthology of Canadian Form Poetry* (Polestar 2005), *Evergreen: Six New Poets* (Black Moss 2002), *You & Your Bright Ideas: New Montreal Writing* (Véhicule 2001), my chapbook *I, Nadja* (above/ground 2000), my chapbook *When Your Body Takes to Trembling* (Cranberry Tree 1996), *Queen's Quarterly*, www.poetics.ca, *Room of One's Own*, *The Antigonish Review*, *PRISM International*, *The Malahat Review*, the *McGill Daily* Literary Supplement, *Propaganda*.

I gratefully acknowledge the support of the Canada Council for the Arts, which assisted in the completion of this work in the form of a grant for Professional Writers and a Travel grant. Poems in the section Equipment for Living were written while I was a Poetry fellow at Hawthornden Castle, Scotland.

Deep thanks to Barry Dempster for his remarkable sense of craft, generosity of spirit, and all the suggestions, insights, and encouragement he offered me in the editorial process.

Thanks, as well, to Kitty Lewis, Maureen Scott Harris and Elizabeth Philips at Brick.

As a participant in the Writing Studio at the Banff Centre for the Arts, I benefited from the advice of Don McKay, John Pass, Barry Dempster and P.K. Page—wonderful poets, readers and teachers, all. I am especially indebted to Don McKay, who taught the only creative writing course I took, in 1988, and who has taught me so much since then.

Other artists of the beautiful have supported and inspired me in countless ways and responded to my work. Thanks to my husband Wes Folkerth, thoughtful reader, my mooring post. Thanks to Masarah Van Eyck—poet, gardener, salt—for the title *Ex Libris*, and myriad other gifts. Thanks to Rachel Rose for her friendship, for her keen eye, for every map. To Brian Trehearne, who offered encouragement and critique on the first Nadja poems. To rob mclennan, who has published my poems, and organized and hosted events where I read them. And to my family.

In addition to Adrienne Rich's lines, "Four Postcards" also references lines by Phyllis Webb and Pier Giorgio di Cicco.

The Nadja poems flowered from my reading of André Breton's surrealist romance, *Nadja*, for me a magical seed. Some of the poems contain a line attributed to Nadja in his book (Richard Howard's translation). I use real names, locations and historical situations, but I also invent details, cultivating and pruning to create a hybrid of fact and fiction in these poems. The usual disclaimers for such works apply. While the majority of the Nadja poems are inventions, written long before I came across jpegs of Nadja's manuscript letters online, "Chez Graff" is a distillation and poetic reconfiguration of one of those letters, written on stationery from the Brasserie of that name. Nadja's letters were purchased by the Bibliothèque Jacques Doucet, Paris, in April 2003. G. Lalo is a French manufacturer of social stationery, founded in 1919 and based in Paris.

Biographical Note

Susan Elmslie's poetry has appeared in several Canadian journals, anthologies, and in a prize-winning chapbook, *When Your Body Takes to Trembling* (Cranberry Tree, 1996). Born in Brampton, Ontario, she currently lives in Montreal with her husband, daughter and, for part of the year, her teenage step-son. She received a PhD in English with a specialization in Canadian literature from McGill University, and has been a poetry Fellow at Hawthornden Castle in Scotland.